Just My Thoughts

D'Ante D.Conover

ISBN: 0615558518
ISBN-13: 978-0615558516

For Booking and Inquiries: Phone: 269-910-6846 Email: TheDeepImpactInc@gmail.com

DEDICATIONS

To my mother and father William and Sandra Hamner-Langford for your commitment in raising me through the adversities and challenges you endured and never stopped believing in me, thank you and I love you. To my brothers and sisters Crystal,Gerald, Randy, and Bill thank you for continuing to reinforce the importance of "family" and continuing to be an integral role in my life. To my Uncle Alfred thank you for all of the trips to the"Detroit Auto Show", the introduction to "Dolby Surround Sound", and all of your guidance. To my Uncle Winifred thank you for always stressing the importance of education and all of the trips that you made to Detroit over the years to spend time with our family. To John and Holly Spitzner for being so kind, loving and encouraging Holly thank you for your contributions to this work and your expertise, I don't know how I could have done it without you. Thank you to the "Urban Blend Coffee House" for believing in me every step of the way (Mr and Mrs. Parker, Marquitte Anderson). James Robinson "my brother" and business partner thank you for all of the encouragement and support over the years and taking the risk to do the JRDC venture with me. To all of my supporters I thank you without you there is no me. To everyone that I did not get to mention thank you for anyway that you have contributed to my life.

CONTENTS

ACKNOWLEDGMENTS

The Urban Blend Coffee House (Kalamazoo, Michigan)
Rosebed Productions
Deep Impact Radio
G.v.s.u. NAACP Chapter President Kalena Lashan

By: D'Ante D. Conover

"MASTERPIECE IN DETROIT"

Imagine being broken only to be rebuilt.
See my faith has me tied together with the strength of a
cuban link.
I'm from the city where drug trafficking and Cartier glasses are
somewhat idols.
But I still loved rapping, the stress and the pressure was like
having a car on 22's or maybe 24's.
The plateau effect of being trapped inside with a tech on the
dresser.
So cold and gloomy amongst regular competitors I still shined,
I was broken but still strong light skinned and added swag
from the "Azzaro Chrome" cologne,
kept the ladies in the zone. I was in a paradise trying to
overcome the visions of street politics
and hustlers with a pair of dice, mean while my people dying
over a pair of Nikes.
See when you evolve from the urban mental constraints of
being mentally restrained,
you have a universal mindset and you become literally
retrained but that knowledge of how rough city life is forever
retained
Shit never changes in the D but the sacrifices without
consequence.
People without common sense trying to purchase malt liquor
with half an id,
would be highly unlikely in Kalamazoo, these folks are radical.
Surrealism is realism in a city plagued by corruption,

but I love the D the art, the music, the culture, the late night
coney island visits.
I still have my peripheral scanning, I have an eye for suspicion
this is my masterpiece, my Vangogh, my Da vinci, my
Rembrandt, my Jean Michel Basquiat, My Andy Warhol,the
art of my mind painting these images in war-time.

By: D'Ante D. Conover

"STOP COMPLAINING"

Are you in debt? broke? or no job?

Stop complaining!

Are you eating, sleeping, waking up to another day no matter the weather conditions?

Stop complaining!

Self-control is wealth! Moderation is dire to your mental,physical, and spiritual health,

so stop complaining!

We take for granted the choices, the options, God has given us!

Why immerse yourself in materialism? to only live in the obliteration, the self-destruction of yourself.

The obstacle is being self-conscience about things of unimportance.

Stop complaining!

If you don' know who you are take time to find yourself.

To the youth, the truth is in your initiative and your drive to see beyond the vision of the naked eye,

because the only promise of reaching that limit of the sky comes from the faith inside.

Stop complaining!

Racial tension will continue, facial expressions will continue to frown as you reach that inner-peace,

but that crab in the barrel effect doesn't have to affect your progress.

Don't speak of your accolades be modest.

Don't lie to yourself be honest.

For there is purity in the truth.

Will you continue to let the ganja effect your conscience?

Will you walk that treacherous mountain, with minimal resources barefoot?

"Life is a recipe and we are the chefs"

We accumulate our ingredients, through our experiences, our willingness to accept, ability to forgive, compassion for others and a universal mindset,

to make that first class meal of humility.

Stop complaining! and take control of what you have.

Utilize and compensate for what you don't have, and that treacherous mountain could soon become a smooth path.

By: D'Ante D.Conover

"GOD MADE ME A SOLE PROPRIETOR"

God made me a sole proprietor! In the midst of the storm he gave me the ability to make choices ,to build a business that builds businesses, to live the American dream.

God made me a sole proprietor! to contract myself, to use my inner wealth, to make choices that affect my health and to better myself. I am the boss off me!

I have the ability, to write life checks and cash them, to take risks and laugh at them.

My decisions are board of director actions.

God made me a sole proprietor! to be my own staff, to grab within grasp, the foundations of excellence he has set in my path.

To motivate for longevity and success, **God made me a sole proprietor!**

to form partnerships, to overcome competition and to avoid adverse hardships, no matter how hard it gets, to explore the uniqueness of my potential, to certify my growth, through my experiences to build credentials and to live my life simple **God made me a sole proprietor!**

and has given me the ability to present this info.

By: D'Ante D. Conover

"WHATS LOVE GOT TO DO WITH IT"

What's love got to do with it?

My people are heart-broken, because they have chosen incompatible souls to comfort them,

instead of following what their hearts have chosen.

Instinct is intertwined in our mind, body, and souls

to move and navigate that indecisive ocean that they must cross, to reach that #1 goal

called companionship.

Whats love got love to do with it?

if you have that "much coveted" baddest chick,

whats beneath those pedicured toes, and lips that glow

may surprise you. In order to have a relationship,

personality must have consistent flow and consistent growth.

Whats love got to do with it ladies?

when that man with a plan, doesn't have a plan that includes you,

when he is the only one rocking fly clothes and you struggle to buy diapers for your baby and live frugal

and breakfast , lunch, and dinner is ramen noodles and desert is dry fruit loops.

Whats love got do with it?

when a friend can never lend an ear, unless you purchase a beer,

and the only purpose of their existence, is to lurk in the silhouette of your shame and to cheer because you live in fear.

Whats love got to do with it?

when your peers can never deliver in the workplace,

and their excuse of lack of productivity, is because no one acknowledged "that hurt face",

now tell me if it really mattered in the first place?

Whats love got to do with it?

When that doctor tells you your child has a birth defect,

and you scream "malpractice!" and say they showed you the worst respect.

Whats love got to do with it?

tell me tell me!, I'm listening, this goes to show, how love sometimes has no effect!

By: D'Ante D. Conover

"NOSTALGIA"

The undertone and presentation of novelty items at the dollar store.
The importance of earplugs, with one functioning ear bud to get us through our day of agony,

but one-sided yes! one-sided! "Hard ass burritos"! and fake ass "Hot Pockets"! in freezers
labeled "We accept Ebt!"
is nostalgia yes nostalgia!
and then there is the old and young sheep occupying aisles like "Occupy Wall Street",

mismatching dinnerware, in excitement for "two for a dollar specials".

Next, we head to toys where little boys rip open, the imitation "Transformer Toys" and say
"Mama Mama!" "Can I get this?"

Oh! you see the the "working class peoples", attitude really start to get in to this "I'm going to
splurge mentality"

Every purchase made, is yet another tragedy!, for not purchasing "American made".
This is nostalgia yes nostalgia!
We approach hardware, gathering hard stares, from handymen, with no clue how to fix anything.

They buy screwdrivers and hammers and they break! and they come back and buy screwdrivers
and hammers, believing that, "they saved a buck".

I somehow found my way to candy, where old men fight, over the assorted butterscotch and
spearmint. I then realize, there's a woman with a head scarf chanting "Girl they got Godiva
Chocolate" when really its, "good diver chocolate".

Her smile and candor could sell water to a whale.

I then reach "checkout" and I'm literally ready to check out.

This mental maze of confusion that, "I got a good deal" is nostalgia I tell you nostalgia!

By: D'Ante D. Conover

"THE BLACK HOLE"

I have disconnected from the pro-black persona.
I have lived amongst the most crime ridden communities.
I have seen destruction and death.
I have seen a renaissance in a city plagued by drugs and ignorance.
I have rocked crowds and watched others jock styles.
I have excelled past my potential.
I have lost track of my accolades, and credentials.
I have become stagnated, in a black hole feeling alone and helpless at times.
I continue to breathe!
I continue to work!
I yearn to inspire just one in a million, even though I am one in a million.
I am not a diamond
I am the rocks blasted into diamonds,
the raw, the unpredictable literary messenger!
Yes this is me!
The blue collar worker, trying to hustle a few dollars to survive and sustain,to move forward, not
for financial gain, but evolution yes evolution!

I want out! I want out of this complacency!

This black hole is far to much!

By: D'Ante D. Conover

"MAKE A STATEMENT"

Make a statement and take a stand for how you feel.

Encased in this sea of pity recreate and re-emerge to greatness.

Your lifestyle is la vida loca! so your life's wild!

Make a statement to educate your self, segregate yourself from the ignorance,

that the media portrays only to brainwash you.

Don't be programmed become the programmer.

You can see how enthusiastic cliches of hope will guide you,

see that inner-faith and that moral compass is your conscience speaking to you.

Make a statement to effect the masses.

Thoughts of poverty, loss of property, block your thoughts,

like jammed traffic.

Poetic justice to me is a habit.

Put your-self on that plateau because you are "God's" child.

Make a statement, to become that king or queen,

whether you sing or scream.

Let it be known that the "Devil" has lost.

Your are your own boss. We claim a victory on negativity no matter the cost.

Make a statement, to become that man or woman others aspire to be.

Its powerful even dreaming, because those dreams become visions, and

those visions if applied will never die.

By: D'Ante D.Conover

"ANTICIPATION IS DESIGNATION"

We are on the playing field called life.

Some people want to test the waters until the umpire calls out.

Anticipation is designation when you can create your own plays.

Dreaming is artwork, when you the person creates ways to get paid.

With the use of the mind, we are no longer locked behind obstacles. We are engulfed in a society, where technologically anything is possible.

Anticipation is designation, when that assumption of slaves, whips and chains prevails.

What do we do a as colored folks?

Go buy whips and chains!

And live in literally hell?

Anticipation is designation, when the good and the bad becomes, the fruit your tree will bear.

We are so self-conscience about things of unimportance.

Instead of sharing our excess, we'd rather waste and hoard un-needed portions.

How can we blame, the faults of one man, to have claimed our right, to place a stake on fame and our ability to sustain.

Anticipation is designation,

when you see and believe only what is within your immediate environment,

and we the people are constantly talking retirement?

The exploitation of our women and children.

We as men are responsible,

for this onslaught its sickening.

"LOVELY LADY"

Compassion for a kindred spirit,
and a beautiful soul.

Oh! how she swayed those thick hips and commanded even the most lost souls.
Millionaires and ball players alike, all dressed to impressed.

She never had succumb to the celebrity sites.
She stood statuesque, proud and with pride.
Her eyes as cunning ,as a lion claiming its prize.
Her intelligence, and aura all tuned into this gorgeous package,

had me envisioning, her measurements, into a proportionate fashion.

She was in fact fashion, the trend setter's trendsetter, that knew how to dress, no matter the weather.

Oh what a lovely lady! Indeed a lovely lady!

"RE-INVENT YOU"

There's a lot of frustration in finding yourself.
Credit scores, criminal records, and employee performance
reports do a lot to your reputation.
But who are you?
In the event, you are one of the above mentioned,
inhale for a moment, and pause! Now exhale let it all out!!
We may not be, the monster that we are so proclaimed to be.
For we as people are preyed upon, without proper education,
to defeat that one enemy called "ignorance".
Reinvent you by taking the time to listen, be assertive, be
observant, and never take no for an answer.
There is always a way! The tenacity in one's actions,
prove that there is justice, in the very word you speak.
Don't build expectations, based upon another person's
character, build a foundation of becoming your own expectation.
We transpose to transcribe, visions of becoming something
greater then that so called "average person".
We vibe with the harmony of choruses, that encourage
alternative lifestyles, of one night stands, and popping bottles of rozay without,
having a plan to sustain with the possibility of having a child.
Reinvent you for the cause of humanity, for the productive
output, and the ability to set an example.
Drake said "Would have came back for you!, I just needed time
to do what I had to do" What if doing what I had to do was just bad news? What
if that very thought, of being a pimp or player, cost me my life just because I
wanted to make the action news?
The consequence of doing the same thing twice, is not just a
mistake, but a designation of becoming a victim of your own fate.
Reinvent your purpose, analyze the music videos before you
get hype to Hype Williams, or spend your whole night making it rain dollar

bills, make it rain opportunity, and exercise your mind to intelligence.
Our children are prone to Aston Martin Music, yet they
struggle to do math and worry about not what is right but what is popular the
destruction of ourselves as we speak is our work in progress.

By: D'Ante D. Conover

"TIME"

What does time imply?
The effect and manifestation of, bringing life into existence and frequently those that cease to exist.
Time is an early release capsule of medication, that society uses to deem urgency.
Not many baby's fathers, and baby's mothers consider how the two minutes of pleasure, and exertion of sweats, bodily fluids, and penned up energy result in the creation of a child
Not many gamblers betting their life savings, on a Black Jack table consider the five minutes, they spent blowing 10,000 dollars will effect their lifestyle.
Time is that void and precious moment we use to avoid our reality.
Time is the one or two seconds between fame and tragedy.
What does time imply?
We spend our lives striving to live grand, through shortcuts, and pyramid scams only to realize thy we have scammed ourselves.
Time is how we prioritize our health, to buy more time, for what though? some for success, and some for failure,some for growing old and becoming knowledgeable elders, some for rich and some for poor, either way it goes time is never guaranteed to us ,even if we desire more!

.

By: D'Ante D. Conover

"A FATHER'S TRIBUTE"

THERE ARE THINGS I WANT TO SAY TO YOU
THAT ARE DIFFICULT TO VOICE
I AM YOUR PRODUCT, WITH YOUR VALUES
MORALS, AND FREEDOM OF CHOICE
I TRY TO CHOOSE WELL,
ALTHOUGH AT TIMES IT'S HARD
THAT IS WHEN I REACH FOR YOUR GUIDANCE,
YOUR STRENGTH, AND YOUR LOVE.
YOUR FAITH, BELIEFS, BELIEFS AND WISDOM I HIGHLY REGARD
AT DIFFERENT TIMES IN LIFE WE ARE MILES APART,
AND THAT IS WHEN THE DISTANCE BETWEEN US
IS JUST A BEAT OF THE HEART.

By: Holly Spitzner

"SHADOW LAND"

SHADOW LAND HAS PASSED AWAY.
IT'S DEATH SHALL NOT BE MOURNED.
OUT OF THE DARKNESS AND INTO THE LIGHT.
NEW FREEDOM TO EXPLORE.
PRAISE THE LORD FOR THE GIFT OF LIFE.
WHERE SHADOWS REIGN NO MORE.
DAWN WASHES CLEAN THE MOON-LESS NIGHT
LIFTING A HEART TO BE REBORN.
GRACIOUSLY, SINGS A DORMANT SPIRIT
THAT HAS AWAKENED AT LONG LAST.
CRUSHING THE CHAINS, AND BREAKING THE HOLD
OF THE DARK NIGHT OF THE SOUL
PRAISE THE LORD FORE IT HAS COME TO PASS,
SHADOW LAND IS DEAD!

By: Holly Spitzner

"GRANDMOTHER"

IN ALL THE UNADULTERATED BEAUTY.
THERE IS A LIFE OF IT'S OWN.
HERE THE PRESENCE IS FELT EMPIRICALLY,
ONLY THROUGH THE SENSES IT IS KNOWN.
ALTHOUGH IT IS NOT TANGIBLE,
YOU CAN FEEL IT.
WHEN SHE REACHES OUT TO CARESS,
IN THE WARMTH OF THE SUN, CAN BE SEEN IN THE SKY,
HER FRAGRANCE IS IN THE BREEZE,
WHEN THE DAY IS NEARLY DONE.
DURING QUIET HOURS HER WHISPER IS HEARD,
IN THE SOUND OF THE WAVES LAPPING THE SHORE.
I FEEL SO CLOSE TO HER,
EVEN THOUGH THERE ARE NO SPOKEN WORD.
YET, THE DISTANCE IS GREAT.
MEANWHILE, THE SEAGULLS SOAR,
AND THE BIRCH TREES RATTLE THEIR LEAVES.
HER LOVE IS SHOWERED OVER ME.

ABOUT THE AUTHOR

D'Ante D. Conover, a product of Detroit, Michigan was raised on the city's northwest side to a devoted, loving, and hard-working middle-class family (William and Sandra Hamner-Langford). Early on in his youth, D'Ante took to the likings of reading "National Geographic Magazines" and science fiction books, after being exposed to them at age five by his late grandfather Hosea Alfred Hamner. D'Ante went on to develop, a love for reading periodicals,novels, poetry and short stories and anything that he could get his hands on. D'Ante hails from a "family of entertainers" with strong ties to the "Motown Music Era", receiving guidance from Motown Records legend "Carolyn Crawford" and many others during his teen years. At age 14, he received his first "Sony Walkman" as a Christmas gift, which then sparked another passion "rap music" which eventually lead to him being a fixture on the "Detroit Rap Scene". "I borrowed my brother's Jay-z cd and started memorizing the lyrics and reciting them in the mirror." "You couldn't tell me, nothing I was a rapper and that's all there was to it." "In 2001, I had already written three notebooks, of lyrics and carried them around faithfully like the "Bible" sharing them with other aspiring teenage rappers at my school". By, early 2002 D'Ante recorded, several independent albums with Seven Strikes Entertainment and had signed a management contract with Smiley Entertainment Management, but eventually all became halted over management conflicts and money issues. "I was completely disheartened, I never wanted to record another record again, but the fast-paced lifestyle and all of the broken promises just didn't suit me, so I just quit". In 2005, D'Ante re-emerged onto the music scene becoming, a regular on the rap battle circuit only to become discouraged again. D'Ante relocated to Kalamazoo, Michigan in 2007 to pursue his education at Western Michigan University. "I spent a few years going to school, working full-time and in and out of relationships, so I began to write about my life experiences, this became my therapy and my escape from the day to day stresses of life". "In 2010, a really good friend, Marquitte Anderson informed me that her family was opening a coffee shop in town". "Marquitte told me, that they were having an open mic and I just couldn't resist". "Now was the time, to share with the world my thoughts, I had already written "rap's, so I figured how hard could it be to write a poem". D'Ante ,began to perform regularly at the "Urban Blend Coffee House" which eventually led to being invited to other venues. "In the middle of 2010, I got a call from a long-time friend (James Robinson) stating "man you need to write a book I'm going to email you the info", and from that point on, I was not just a poet, I had became an author".

Guest Writer: Holly Sue Spitzner

Holly Schwoebell Spitzner was born and raised in Kalamazoo, Michigan, her love of poetry was inspired, at an early age by her mother Ruth C. Webb Schwoebell who frequently read poetry to her children. Holly, started writing poetry as a young woman, it became the instrument, for her to cope with life as she knew it. Holly has four children and a loving, devoted husband John Spitzner. "When I met Holly I couldn't believe, how much of an incredible person she was". "After, sharing some of my poetry with her, she then told me me she also wrote poetry, I was thinking to myself no way!, the first piece she read to me "Shadow Land", just blew me away, and from that point on I knew that I wanted to work with her on a book." -"D'Ante D. Conover". Already, a nationally published poet Holly, has re-emerged yet again bringing her life experiences, passion, and astute intelligence to the forefront of the poetry world.